Tales of the Supernatural

Also by Maura Stanton

POETRY

Cries of Swimmers (1984)
Snow on Snow (1975)

FICTION

Molly Companion (1977)

Tales

of the

Supernatural

Poems by

Maura Stanton

David R. Godine
Publisher · Boston

for Richard

First published in 1988 by
David R. Godine, Publisher, Inc.
Horticultural Hall
300 Massachusetts Avenue
Boston, Massachusetts 02115

LC: 88-45331
ISBN: 0-87923-749-X
ISBN: 0-87923-750-3 (pbk.)

First Edition
Printed in the United States of America

Acknowledgment is made to the following publications, where some of the poems in this book first appeared:

The American Poetry Review: "The Tidal Wave," "Inside the Alp," "Wasps"; *Chelsea*: "Paradise," "Persephone," "Diana and Her Companions"; *Crazyhorse*: "Good People," "Overnight in St. Louis"; *Kentucky Poetry Review*: "The Angry Ballerina"; *The Louisville Review*: "Polio Epidemic, 1953," "The Invalid in the Window"; *The Michigan Quarterly Review*: "The Dance"; *The Missouri Review*: "The Grocery Store"; *Ploughshares*: "The Cuckoo Clock," "Attendant Lord," "Heaven," "Space," "March"; *Poetry*: "Modern Lives," "Pole Vaulting," "Wander Indiana," "Living Apart"; *Seneca Review*: "Trees, Trees"; *The Sierra Madre Review*: "The Headache"; *Telescope*: "Sorrow and Rapture"; *Verse*: "The Village of the Mermaids".

"Good People" was reprinted in *New American Poets of the 80's*, Wampeter Press and in *Strong Measures: Contemporary American Poetry in Traditional Forms*, Harper & Row; "Sorrow and Rapture" was reprinted in *The Pushcart Prize, X*, The Pushcart Press; and "The Cuckoo Clock" was reprinted in *The Ploughshares Poetry Reader*, Ploughshares Press.

I would like to thank the Indiana Arts Commission for a fellowship that helped me to complete this collection.

Contents

I

Tales of the
Supernatural

During the first year that Mr. Wordsworth and I were neighbors our conversations turned frequently on the two cardinal points of poetry, the power of exciting the sympathy of the reader by a faithful adherence to the truth of nature, and the power of giving the interest of novelty by the modifying colors of imagination. The sudden charm which accidents of light and shade, which moonlight or sunset diffused over a known and familiar landscape, appeared to represent the practicability of combining both. These are the poetry of nature. The thought suggested itself (to which of us I do not recollect) that a series of poems might be composed of two sorts. In the one, the incidents and agents were to be, in part at least, supernatural; and the excellence aimed at was to consist in the interesting of the affections by the dramatic truth of such emotions as would naturally accompany such situations, supposing them real. And real in *this* sense they have been to every human being who, from whatever source of delusion, has at any time believed himself under supernatural agency. For the second class, subjects were to be chosen from ordinary life; the characters and incidents were to be such as will be found in every village and its vicinity where there is a meditative and feeling mind to seek after them, or to notice them when they present themselves.

—SAMUEL TAYLOR COLERIDGE
Biographia Literaria

The Tidal Wave

Today the window pane is starred with ice.
The map of Ireland glitters in the frost
And from my bed I watch the sun dissolve
The little flakes I call the western coast.
I walked there as a boy, my life a dream,
Ungraspable as clouds, a mystery
I thought I'd pass into as I grew up
Like a boat on course gliding into fog.
One day I sailed out to America
In darned socks, and my father's mended suit.
My arm ached in the socket as I waved
Goodbye to every disappearing face.
Now my past is a cloud, faint and shapeless—
The packed-in feathers of my old pillow
Are all I feel beneath my heavy head.
My birthdate's carved into polished granite
Next to the name and death date of my wife.

A caretaker will give my son a map
To find our graves if he forgets the place.
A mower, taking off his sweaty shirt,
May cool his back against the grey headstone,
May read my name aloud, and speculate
About the man from Ireland buried here
So far from home, in view of skyscrapers.
And what will be the difference to me?
When I was ten I loved a neighbor girl.
We used to climb a hillside where sheep grazed,

Sit on a stone wall, and stare at the sea,
Talking shyly. She used to bite her nails,
Or comb the tangles out of her black hair.
Sometimes we shut our eyes against the wind.
Our lives were equal then. We'd both grow up.

That spring her family drove to Castlebar.
The blackest storm old men had ever known
Rose from the sea when they were almost home.
The horse could hardly step. The baby cried.
I used to dream of what I never saw,
The mother with her shawl, the little girl
Grabbing her father's arm as the horse reared.
It was too dark to see the wave curl up
And cross the beach, the low dunes, and the road,
To smash them like an iron battering-ram.
Deep-sea fish writhed in the farmers' fields
Next day, but no one found the cart or horse.
The whole family had been dragged to sea.

For years I walked the beach, wondering
If she might wash ashore. I was afraid
Of dark seaweed floating under the surf.
Then I forgot, and sailed above her grave,
Thinking about New York, jobs, and money.
She was a tale I told, an old story.
She has no monument, no name in stone.
She's undistinguished, nothing more than foam.

But who am I? My life has vanished, too.
My son will choose one of my baggy suits
To bury my corpse in, give the rest away.
A granddaughter may someday speak of me,
Then comes oblivion. I'll melt like ice.
Already on the sunny windowpane
My map of Ireland has begun to run
In speeding droplets down the empty glass.

Wander Indiana

Introduced in January 1984, the "Wander"
plates have been a cause for much unhappiness
and confusion—not only for Indiana residents,
but also for motorists around the country. . . .
Some thought "Wander" was a county—a large
one—somewhere in central Indiana.
                    —Newspaper Editorial

How did I come to be here? I suppose
I was like other girls at first, just shyer.
I used to stand outside the practice room
Listening to Chopin on the piano
With my eyes closed, imagining love.
I was a wise man in the Christmas play,
No lines to speak, but the whole stage to cross
Pretending to follow a light-bulb star.
I liked to spin the globe in my homeroom
After school, and stop it with my finger.
Then I grew up, got glasses, read thick books.
I saw the sights that all explorers see
When I began to travel, yet somehow
The pictures in the books were always brighter—
"Smiling mermaids, combing their yellow hair"
The caption said, but when I reached that shore
And saw the mermaids sprawled upon their rocks,
I saw how thin they were, how they shivered,
And tried to dry their wet tails with their hair.

I heard the rumors about Shangri-la:
Yes, most of them are true, the palms sway
And gentle unicorns crop the green grass
Below the snow-capped, shadowy mountains,

But people stopped me on broad avenues
To ask me a question: Was I ever happy
Down there where snow fell? If I said "Yes,"
They turned from me in shock, almost angry,
Swept up their gauzy robes, and walked away.
That's when I crossed the Iceberg Sea to Limbo
And disembarked in the ramshackle port.
It looked so ordinary, a town of bars
And rutted streets. Inside the "Rainy Daze"
I asked a sailor if he ever tried
To catch a glimpse of Heaven through the fog.
He shook his head, lifting his heavy stein.

But it was on my short voyage to Hell
That I first heard of Wander, Indiana.
I waited on the shore beside the Lethe
Among the mingling shades. I had no right
To passage on the ferry for the dead,
And the shades jostled me, mocking, annoyed.
I was loveless, hopeless, but I was alive,
Solid enough to weight the buoyant wood
Of the deck, remind them of their losses.
After the ferryman refused to take me
I pleaded with the dead. Where should I go?
Wander, Indiana some voices hissed
Above the groan of oars, the shrieks and moans.
And so I drove across the big prairie
Searching for the narrow road to Wander.

The sky was blue, the rustling corn uncut.
I passed the quarry and the water tower,
Drove into the county seat at twilight—
It looked real. I knew that strangers slept
Soundly at the Bide-a-Wee Motel,
Then drove away, never suspecting the trick:
The whole town, the whole enormous county,
Is made of drifting vapor, molecules
Combined—no one knows how—to resemble
Shapes of houses, hardware stores, and people.
None of us exist. We're clouds of matter
Driven by gusts of passion, lips dissolving
As we smile at you, and give you directions.

Two White Hens

I owned a little shack
Not far from the Pacific
Where I grew broccoli.
I liked to sit on my porch
Beside my two white hens,
All I loved in the world,
And talk to wrinkled men
In black rain-slickers
About the ends of the earth.
Sometimes they drew maps
Deep in my fresh dirt
With their mahogony canes,
Turning up glistening snails
As they marked the Iceberg Sea
Or traced the shortest route
To Bangkok or Bahia.
During the winter storms
I watched the waves arrive
Big as the walls of churches.
Later I touched the kelp
Darkening on the rocks,
Imagining a forest
Under the dome of water.
I stared at red starfish,
Anemone, and chitons
Caught in shallow tide pools
That formed between storms,
And felt dissatisfied

As if I, too, were clinging
Like a mussel to a rock,
Shut in my own fastness.
So I dreamed of distant places
Bored by my tall fir trees,
The fog that blew in and out,
My stove, teapot, garden.
I grew so thin and sad
My hens clucked nervously.
Even today I recall
How they'd fly after me
On short, useless wings,
Opening their yellow beaks,
Alarm in their black eyes.
Oh, I can hardly tell
My story—
My jaw is stiff with grief.
I sold my shack to strangers,
Packed up my books and cups,
Then crated up my hens.
I took a ship that foundered
Out on a coral reef,
And as we began to go under
I released the little hens,
Then dove into the surf
Where sailors gasped and churned,
Trying to reach the sand
Just beyond the breakers.

One of eight survivors,
Half-strangled, exhausted,
Living on seaweed broth,
I watched the sky for days
But dared hope for nothing
As I heard the sailors talk
Of eating my poor hens
If they should wash ashore.
Sometimes a cloud arrived,
Feathery, shaped like wings,
And I'd hide my eyes.
Yes, I was rescued at last.
I saw the marble cities,
All I'd longed to see,
Lisbon, Amsterdam . . .
I sailed to the top of the earth
Where the monotonous snow
Falls through endless night.
Now I'm a wrinkled woman.
I wear a yellow slicker
And rage at the heaving waves
I once desired to cross.
Sometimes at the top of a breaker
I think I see my hens . . .
Oh, foolish, fond woman,
Love turns again to foam!

The Headache

I was sitting in a chair with my headache,
Wishing for something heartfelt and contagious
To come in the mail, to telephone, or knock.
I had my hands over my eyes.
I tried to pull the pain up from my brain
But the brain cared nothing for my touch.
It was listening to Schubert
Played on the violin next door
By a red-haired girl
To whom I've never spoken, although her window
On the second floor is opposite my window.
Sometimes our cats look out at one another.

The music entered my brain. I felt the sparks.
The notes made asterisks on the wet mass
Folded into the chamber of my skull,
Which I could see when I looked inward.
Soon I grew to expect a little phrase
Made up of perfect sounds, which returned
Again and again to match a wave of pain
That jolted like a zigzag of lightning
Across my cortex, into the cerebellum.

It might have looked like sleep, but it wasn't.
I knew I was in a chair. I felt the cushions.
Schubert came up the stairs in an old coat
And stood beside me, his hands on his temples.
His brain was a level, and inside

Pain floated like a bubble.
He kept it centered on the crooked world.
I watched him rocking in his boots, humming
As he invented the mournful andante
Meant to pierce the heart of anyone.
I think I called to him. But he was gone.
The girl next door stopped playing.
Then I got up. My headache wasn't cured
But for a day I kept my brain from thinking
About its curled and tender hemispheres.

The Grocery Store

At first I used to read headlines
At check-out stands with a laugh:
WOMAN CAPTURES SHRIEKING GHOST,
Or else, SHIP RETURNS FROM LIMBO.
I only wanted what I saw,
Apples, ginger root, and beans,
Or gleaming flasks of vinegar.
I didn't need a mystery world
Where spirits knocked, or aliens
Landed in a humming saucer.
I drove to shop past fields of corn,
Saw the corn turned to stubble,
And never thought of death in fall
But only of the Christmas hams.
Then one day the produce man,
A neighbor I had known for years,
Wept to say his wife had died
By her own perverse desire,
Locked inside their big garage.
I stood near him at the funeral.
He told me she was not in heaven
But only somewhere in the air
Just beyond our narrow vision.
Later he spoke about a séance.
Friends had held his sweating hands.
He called his wife until she rapped
A message on the table top.
The medium whispered in the dark:

Yes, she loves you tenderly
But she trembles with the cold.
Light a candle and she'll come.
So every night he lights a candle
And he feels the faint rustle
As she steps in from the dark
To scorch her invisible hands.

• • •

Every week the garish headlines
Insist there is another world
That ordinary people see—
Spaceships land in backyards;
A baby cures a multitude;
An angry ghost destroys the china
To the amazement of a waitress;
A dentist shouts from his coffin—
For even when we die there's still
Hope for revenge, or true love.
Deep inside my chest I feel
Blood moving through the arteries.
Sometimes I'm dizzy when I stand.
I know my body's nothing more
Than a side of beef in the freezer,
Mapped, ready for cutting.
But when I wait at the register
At busy times, I seem to feel
Some buzz or hum or energy

Coming from the hands in motion,
Talking mothers, businessmen,
Old women buying bran flakes,
Teenagers in line with pizzas—
Everyone reads the shocking news,
Silently, or to a friend,
Eyebrows moving in irony
Or lips in private wonder,
And on every stranger's face
I see a flash of agony:
Why not? Why not a miracle?

The Village of the Mermaids

after Paul Delvaux

Why did the old men see them, not the young?
At first I listened idly to drunk captains
Describing mermaids over foaming beer.
I waited tables then. I'd see their hands
Twisting as they described the shining tails
To laughing younger sailors, and each swore
Next time he'd jump into those marble arms
Uplifted from the waves. I questioned them.
I stuck a pin into my ocean charts
For each bright face they claimed they saw emerge,
And after many years I knew the route.
My hair was white, my children grown and gone,
My husband dead. I hired an old ship
And set out with my untrustworthy crew
To find the mermaids, famed to live forever.

At night in my cabin, while the sailors
Caroused below me—playing cards, dancing—
I thought about my puzzling life, a dream
Behind me, no more real than a shadow.
Where was the man I'd married? I recalled
The plain of olive trees behind my house,
Some distant, dusty-colored granite mountains,
Specks of people down a road, but every
Blink of my eyes told me it was false—
My past was a mirage. It shone and wavered,
And specters walked inside me, feigning shapes
Of those I loved until I moaned aloud
And tried to grasp a nonexistent hand.

My crew mutinied near the Iceberg Sea
Demanding we turn back. When I refused
They let me down in a wooden lifeboat
With provisions, and I spread out my chart
And rowed east toward the towering icebergs,
Some dense and cloudy, others light as glass.
A strange current pulled me to a crack
That split the largest iceberg. I drifted in—
The sun came angling through the mighty ice
So I could see, though dimly. I didn't care
Where I was, whether awake or asleep.
But then the tunnel opened wide for me;
I shot out on a little rapids, to find
The Village of the Mermaids just ahead.

I saw a thousand mermaids on the beach
Arched on their stomachs, waving graceful arms.
Some came swimming toward me in the water.
I grasped my oar, then looked down at their faces
Bobbing around me. They seemed sweet and mild.
They drew my boat to shore. I was afraid
Of slipping on broken shells as tails thrashed
Around my shaking legs. Up in the Village
More mermaids sat on chairs in long dresses.
I couldn't see their tails or purple gills—
They looked human, pretending to breathe air.
"Welcome," they said in small, flutelike voices.
"Tell us the story of your human life.
We'll sing it back to you in perfect verses."

I had to catch my breath if I had breath.
So this was what I'd come for. My heart beat.
I sat down on an empty chair. I told
What I knew. And then the twangling voices
Spun it into a decorated tale
That made me gasp. I saw my father come
Across the water on a ferryboat,
Laughing from the rail. My mother waved.
The dark-haired man I'd married disembarked.
I reached to stop him in the moving crowd
But he kept on. Too soon I was alone.
I saw the icebergs rising up around me.
"Stop!" I cried, covering my ears.
"You sing too quickly, go back, go back again
To the beginning." I heard the voices hush.
"Your song is over. It is ours to keep."
The mermaids smiled a stiff, archaic smile.
"Now you may disappear with swarming millions
That fill the sea, changing and dissolving."

Wasps

When children knocked and pressed their flat faces
Against the sagging screen, she ran upstairs
To hide inside her room, that child I was,
Preferring the privacy of boredom.
She liked to look out at the wasps' nest
And lean her elbows on the peeling sill,
While wasps flew past her window, entering
The cone-shaped structure underneath the eaves.
Sometimes a wasp tapped against the glass
Its obscure, troublesome message to itself.
She heard her mother's voice beyond the pane.
The heat made her faint. Dizzy, she watched
The wasps dip, circle, and disappear,
Feelers, and narrow waists, slipping in
To that mysterious interior.
But three or four flew at her eyes instead.
She felt them plunging far into her head,
The sharp, translucent wings opening up
In the dark corridors, wings touching wings,
Then shiny heads, long, quivering bodies,
An independent life deep in her ears.
She heard her name floating on the air
But couldn't answer her brother's happy shout
Until the wasps flew out, satisfied
To leave their pearly eggs for future years.

The Cuckoo Clock

Before I could tell time, I'd sit and wait
For the cuckoo in my mother's wooden clock
To open his red door, and sing "cuckoo."
I never knew how many times he'd sing,
But the song was regular, and a long trill
Gave me a chance to look inside his house
Where it was dark and smelled of sweet pine.
I used to wonder what he did in there
Under the curlicues of his painted roof.
I guessed he had a parlor, and two chairs
Pulled up before a real brick fireplace.
He drank tea from thin, china cups,
Smeared honey on his crackers, wiped his beak,
And thought of ways he might invite me in.
Though I was large, I was his favorite.
There was no other reason to appear
So often in our kitchen, where the noise
Of younger brothers rose against my ears.
But I couldn't shrink. Too soon I knew
How long an hour lasted, and I climbed
Up on a kitchen chair and pulled the door
Open before it was time for him to sing.
I saw the mechanism, how he fitted
Neatly on his spring above the gear wheel;
And afterwards he ordered me to bed,

Insisted on time for play and homework.
Then yesterday, standing across the street
From my own house, a grown-up clapboard house,
I had the dizzy feeling that I'd shrunk.
This was the cuckoo's house, though I was forty.
I looked at the red door and the pretty trim.
I was small enough to enter, turn the knob,
Sit down in the other chair before his fire,
Sink back, and rest. Why did I hesitate?
I waited on the curb while cars roared past.
I stared at my door, dismissing fancy,
Then went inside to my familiar rooms.
The fireplace was cold, the tea unmade.
I walked around on rugs and oak floors,
And finally paused before the cuckoo clock,
Which hung in my dining room—the same clock,
A gift from my mother. It had not ticked
For ten years. The iron chains hung still
Beneath the faded, intricate facade
Coated with fine dust. I put my finger
On the door. I wondered if he heard me.
His lintel was so low. And was his floor
A mess of rubble, dirt, feathers, and hair?
I heard him stirring somewhere in the dark
Preparing to greet me, his beak open
Not to sing, but to swallow me at last.

Attendant Lord

I was dressed to be a man
With saggy hose and doublet,
A sword belt, a sword,
And a cap with a ragged feather
Over my pinned-up hair.
I had no lines to speak.
We lords and gentlemen
Standing around in silence,
Cued to swell a progress,
Were played by tall girls.
The short girls were ladies.
During the first scene
I stumbled as I followed
The other lords to the throne.
The audience of parents
On folding chairs in the gym
Clapped at the big speeches.
I heard nothing at all,
Trying to walk straight,
And bow without falling.
Alone in the dressing room
Between acts, I stood
Shaking before the mirror
Recalling my every blunder.
My sword was light and dull.
I held it out before me
As if I might thrust it through
The velvet chest of my image,

Which stared back, unsmiling.
The room was hot and airless.
I was sweating, but cold,
And seemed to be divided,
Coming toward this place,
Perplexed, and transformed
Into a handsome prince
Who scorned my cowardice.
I stepped away from him
And felt, or dreamed I felt,
A sudden shaft of air,
Like a test for glaucoma,
Pressing against my eyes
Wide open and unblinking,
As if some resting spirit,
Wanton, obscure, sexless,
Arose to force entry
Into my distraught brain.
Why return to the play?
No one in that darkness
Beyond the edge of the stage
Would notice I was missing.
The shoulder-rubbing lords
Gathered behind the duke
Would close their ranks.
Let queen and king bow
While curtains rose and fell.
I might stay calmly here,

Thinking of nothing at all,
Needing no praise or blame.
I think I had sunk to my knees
Before I heard the call.
I swear it wasn't me
Who stood up first, but him,
The prince I was in the glass
Who stood up meaning to go
Disguised as me, determined
To finish our bitter role.

Paris

Our first night, almost midnight,
We paused outside the Gare de L'Est
Unfolding our map. We had just arrived,
Hungry, sleepless, preparing for the walk
Into the dark city.

On down the Rue du Faubourg
Past the bumper cars, where young men
In white T-shirts rode around and around
Bumping into their girl friends,
We held hands.
We smelled the burnt rubber, saw the sparks.

A whole city had been conjured up
Out of steam and rock.
We walked through platinum rain
Over bridges, under distinguished trees,
Alone among a million people
Who were not people, only dots of light.

Inside our hotel we shivered.
We thought we had arrived in hell
Accidently with our solid bodies.
We rubbed our thumbs
Over the lion-head finials
Of the glossy, black chair. It seemed to float.
By morning it had weight and measurement.

Today I unfolded my map of Paris—
Now soft and mysterious to the touch
Although its distant streets are familiar—
And searched the abstract plan.
Years have passed. Now I've grown serious.
I know I can still find you

Just as you were, your hair still fine.
I don't need a lyre of gold.
I can pull you up out of the darkness.
I'm holding your hand. Here you are,
Lethean water falling away in drops.

Inside the Alp

I've climbed the inner stairway of the Alp
And stand at last before the cataract
Hidden inside the mountain, where I look
Aghast, dizzy, drinking draughts of spray.
I put both hands on the catwalk's iron rail—
Twenty years ago I hiked this mountain;
I climbed the slope to the edge of the glacier
In summer with my friend, who died last year.
The sun was shining as we walked and talked,
Ate chocolate, photographed the cows,
And tried to separate the mingled bells
Ringing upward from the lower meadows.
I ate my bread and cheese. I counted clouds.
I listened to my friend reciting Wordsworth
And never heard this thundering beneath
The Alpine grass, dotted blue and white
With half-awakened flowers, pure as sleep,
But freshened by this deep, violent source.

Now I hardly see the dark-blue gentians.
I hear thunder under my lightest step.
I stop to pant on ledges. Looking down
On steeples, fields, chalets, I press my heart.
The sky and clouds are far away, unreal.
I've climbed the inner stairway of the Alp,
The stairway built on sleep, that leads to death,
And found at last the secret to myself,
The turbulence, the writhing mist, the fall

Of snow from heights where no one dares to go:
This tumult is the world, my own past.
The cataract inside me swells and swells
As glaciers melt, exposing boulder plains;
The pure and impure waters gather and run
Carrying chunks of ice with the good soil
Over the precipice, down into the dark.
Here comes my friend. I recognize his shape.
I watch the wavering water take him down.

Diana and Her Companions

Vermeer, *oil on canvas*

Now women breathe again.
Tonight's chase is over
And even the spotted dog
Sits and pants awhile.
Diana lifts her foot
Above the metal basin.
She feels the rough sponge
Which her friend is rubbing
Over her chafed skin,
But keeps her face averted.
We don't know what has happened—
Something back in the trees,
A doe shot by mistake,
A man turned into a stag—
But here in the midnight grove
The somber colors speak,
Deep yellow, blue, and orange,
A purple rock, a shadow.

I stare into the painting
Struck by Diana's posture,
And by her chestnut hair
Lit by the tiny crescent
She wears on her deep forehead.
She looks so much like my friend
Who is called Diana, too,
That I am surprised, anxious.
These women are familiar.

I've seen this solemn group
Posed in strange robes before.
One of the five is myself—
The colors swirl together.
I know where I am at last.
Around me are real faces
Drawn by Vermeer's hand
Centuries before they lived.
He caught the downward eye,
The sloping shoulder of grief.
This is the funeral home.
Inside the other room,
Behind the greenish curtain,
Lies Diana's brother
Shot by his own hand.
We are her speechless friends.

Persephone

A small plane shuttles me between two lives,
One real, one false. I fasten the seat belt.
The pilot flies me into autumn gloom
To where my husband lives in flaming mountains.
At night I sleep beside him, hour by hour.
He needs my hands to soothe his heavy brow
And send the shock of life into his heart.
At dawn I walk his streets. I know I hurt
The insubstantial, flickering dead
Who drift forever in his ghostly kingdom—
I show them what they were. I breathe. I step
Through this town they've built out of memory,
And the walls blow away, the turrets fade.

Sometimes I walk down river to the lock
Where water rushes and roars, a smoking wave
That falls back on itself, and goes nowhere.
Upstream the river makes a glassy pond
Where I can see Hell's crimson trees reflected
Deep in the water beyond my living face.
This is eternity. There's gray in my hair.
Some day the pilot will refuse me passage
Back to my other life. I'll spend the spring
In darkness, and my hand against a cheek
Will feel like air . . . Now I ask the dead:
Is this my real life? But they run from me
Just like the white-tailed deer in the forest
Of my other home, terrified that I'm human.

Tunnel of Love

The gypsy claimed she saw
The face of my true love
Deep in her cloudy glass—
I watched her smooth my dollar.
I looked, but saw nothing.
She said I lacked the gift.
Would I meet him today?
He's out there, she said,
If you look without vanity.
I wandered through the fair
Dreamily, looking at men,
Charged with my hope.
I saw the sweating back
Of the Tilt-a-Wheel man;
A father dragging his son
Through a sour-smelling barn
Where newborn lambs trembled
Under their mothers' tongues;
A man with grizzled hair
Forking hay to the cows.
I looked at the cows' eyes,
Lashed, gentle. I shuddered.
I closed my eyes for a moment.
I tried to see the face
Of a movie star, or prince.
Nothing but black dots
Appeared on my inner lids.
At dusk I met my girl friends.

We rode the Ferris wheel,
Holding our dipping stomachs,
Then ate corn dogs, and flirted
With older, college boys
Who gave us cans of beer
And held our sweating hands.
Soon I rode recklessly
Through the Tunnel of Love,
Letting myself be kissed.
Was this love? True love?
I let my fingers slide
Down the neck of the boy
While our boat bumped forward.
Then the skeleton leapt out—
A trick of the management
To get couples to hug
For the eager, waiting crowd—
And I gasped at the skull
Wired invisibly
To let its hinged jaw move,
Shocked as I recognized
Love without Vanity.
Now the ride was over.
Our boat floated out
Through the heart-shaped door.

Tumbleweed

I stand sleepless at the window
Of my brother's house, looking out
Across corn fields at the racetrack
Lit up in tiers like a palace.
The race cars sound like violent wind,
A science fiction storm that shifts
Mountains of dust on other planets—
I hardly know if this is Earth.

Last year I blamed the eerie landscape.
I drove through the Utah desert
While a thunderstorm crowned
Desolate mountains of the moon,
And grain by grain the dust arose
To annihilate the highway.
I saw the tumbleweed approaching
Larger than I ever dreamed,
Bodies the size of my own car
Constructed out of sticks and air.
They hit the windshield, or grill,
Disintegrating under my wheels
While I kept driving sternly forward
Into the invisible distance,
Trying not to gasp, or cringe—
One swerve and I'd find myself
Sinking into an estuary
Of the flooded Great Salt Lake.
Later, at the rest stop,

I drank from the water fountain
Over and over, wiping my mouth,
Then walked out on the white plain.
In ten steps I barely pulled
My shoe out of the heavy salt
That stretched to the curious horizon
Like new snow in the lifting gloom.

I wanted to go east again,
Back to shade trees and fresh rain,
And here I am. Why don't I feel
Comfortable with grassy hills,
Paved streets, and frame houses?
My brother drove me through his town
Pointing out the big racetrack,
The courthouse, his new store,
The restaurant owned by a Greek,
Run-down barns, a massive bull
Ploughing through a yellow pasture.
He drove me across the dam,
Talking about his life, his hopes,
The baby due in another month.
I listened gladly. I was happy.
Still I felt unreal
As if I'd given up my body
Years ago, and rode beside him
Merely as a friendly spirit
Conjured up by his memory.

Now, all at once the races stop,
Startling me with autumn silence.
Then I hear a nearby cricket,
And breezes through the plumed branches.
My brother is sleeping down the hall
Beside his wife and unknown child.
An orange moon rises up,
Just as the racetrack lights go out.
This looks like Earth. I've seen fields
Manured, ready for winter.
I've walked on springy, frosted lawns,
Inhaled woodsmoke, swallowed cider.
Still the horizon seems to tremble
As if I'm at the edge of somewhere
Immense, and dangerous to reach,
The steppes of Mars, a lunar sea.
Any day the wind will howl
And blow me out across that space
Just like those rootless tumbleweed.
Some broke to sticks against my car.
Others whirled along unharmed
Going nowhere, gathering speed.

Space

_____

Monday a boy who cannot lift
Even a hand to wave good-bye
Comes to my office with his mother.

She has pushed him in his wheelchair
As she must have bathed and dressed him,
Clipped his beard, knocked on my door.

Now he tries to speak; he sputters.
Leaning down his mother listens,
Nodding at his urgent noises.

Then she tells me that he writes
Using his teeth to punch out letters
One by one, ten hours a page.

"What is he writing?" Yes, he hears me,
Twisting his face while his eyes shine.
"Another novel," his mother says,

"Space is his setting and his theme,
Stars beyond the firmament."
So she talks on. She makes me see

At once the creatures he prefers
Floating across the dreadful night,
Speechless in their metal casing,

Viewing the universe with wonder—
Silent brains, no flesh, no spine—
Amazing in their goodness, pureness.

All the while his lonely eyes
Behold us as we talk and gesture,
Mother, teacher, aliens, stones.

Newborn Baby Girl Tells of Past Life

National Enquirer (Headline)

I had the shape of nothing, and I lived
With other spirits in the Hidden Valley.
I was invisible, but I existed,
One of the throng that floated here and there
On equal terms with gods and goddesses
Whose substance seemed no different from my own.
I listened to their tales of the human world
Curiously. I thought they made them up.

I heard about the men on ships in storms
Pressing their spears into each other's chests.
So *that* was faithlessness, and *that* betrayal.
Men built towers, then burned the towers down.
They made each other sad, and then they died
Regretting everything. It seemed too strange.
I rested my lightness on the daffodils,
Glad I was hollow, a breeze to step through.

One day a goddess waved a nerveless hand
Into my emptiness. "You're going to change,"
She said. "But I won't. I'll never change.
I'm always going to gleam like sunbeam motes."
She drifted off. I didn't understand her,
Though I'd seen angels when the nubby wings
Cut through their tender shoulder blades, and sent
Them howling to the Dark Woods, home of ghosts.

That day the sun seemed bronze instead of gold.
"Will I grow wings?" I asked a water god
Who looked up at me from a waveless pool,
His hair rippling across the glassy water.
He smiled at me, a different sort of smile.
"It's worse than that," he said. "You'll grow a heart."
Then he slid under leaving only clouds
Reflected on the surface. A fish winked by.

I felt a thickening inside me somewhere
As if I had a space—a length and breadth—
Though I was shadowless, and centaurs still
Galloped through me on their silvery hoofs.
At the edge of the Dark Woods I saw the ghosts
Wringing their weightless hands under the trees.
"Why are you miserable?" I asked. "You're free.
The human world is far below us now."

The nearest ghost stepped forward. I could see
His insubstantial wavering human shape,
Part smoke, part flesh. "You're a new soul," he said.
"Now look into your future: pain and guilt
Await you, then a fading memory—
And only memory will delay extinction."
I saw the throbbing wound burning his chest
Before he fled back to the swampy woods.

I looked across the Hidden Valley then.
I saw a million like me, a million more
Shapeless and pure, soon to be shocked awake.
And then it happened. I felt the descent
Into the body, black and dizzying.
Now I struggle for one last backward view
Before I lose forever that spacious past.
My crib makes bars of shadow over me.

I I

Modern Lives

Modern Lives

When E. divorced his wife, quit his job,
He looked ten years younger, his tie gone,
His hair curly, his car full of presents
For the two kids who lived in another state.
He sent a picture of his smiling girl friend,
Married her, took her to live in Florida,
Where he planned to sell land and know himself.
But now there's panic in his distant voice.
We hear it in his laughter on the phone.
He has no job. He can't pay child support.

He doesn't understand the new computer
And can't be hired back by his old firm.
He's forty-two, his muscles firmer than ever,
And his brain glows. He's reading Kierkegaard,
But his wife won't meet his sincere blue eyes.
He wants us to tell him what life means
Because we're still married, have not yet
Stepped out beyond ourselves into nothing,
Packed a suitcase the way he did, whistling,
And driven away from our familiar chairs.

Wet, yellow leaves, stuck to the sidewalk,
Make a starry pattern under our shoes
As we walk in the mist, talking of E.
So far away, so mysterious to us—
The huge beech tree looming down the street
Is easier to know, rooted in one place.

And so we make comparisons, and think
About your older brother, who disappeared
From his steady job at Bethlehem Steel
And drove his battered truck to Arizona.

I mention S., who gave up his job
Building bridges across Iowa freeways,
And left his homemade cabin in the woods
To live in Houston, unable to bear
The clenching cold that turned supple hands
Into brutish paws. He used to pour
Hot coffee over his hands to wake them up.
Now he dreams of the wilderness he cleared,
Five years of work, sawing, digging a well—
But vines advance, cockroaches, and mice.

And what of H.? We have boxes of letters
Tied up with drying rubber bands, and most
Are from him, raging about his town,
The smallest, ugliest, meanest town on earth,
Where he has lived for twenty lonely years
Without a lover, hardly even a friend.
And Z., who moved reluctantly away
To California, now looks out at palms
And says that sadness is ordinary,
Just like smog, the pall you see through.

We wonder about X. in Birmingham.
She spread a lace cloth on her crooked table
And sipped Scotch from heavy, cut crystal.
Is she still dreaming of a trip to Egypt?
But C., who lived across the alley from me
When we were girls, and played basketball,
Married, and lives in Paris. Now her voice
Sounds odd and shaky when she speaks English.
Did she look up at that white net, and hoop,
And wish she could fly through it like a ball?

Or was it accident? What makes a life?
We've gone around the block a second time,
Past houses, doors, windows, where people live
Sometimes forever, or just until the movers
Come again with their big orange vans.
I see an old man looking out at us—
A strolling couple, part of the landscape.
When he rubs his eyes, and turns away,
I imagine E., wearing his new glasses,
Reading in bed beside a sleeping stranger.

The Angry Ballerina

She talks to herself out loud,
Or talks to me, her hair
Brushed out from her head
The width of two faces.
Her thick eyebrows quiver.
She moves her fists to music
When the orchestra begins
Tchaikovsky's *Nutcracker*,
And sits upright, rigid,
Partly blocking my view
When the red curtain opens.
She's barely sixteen, I think,
But her face is white, ageless.
She hates all that she sees:
The girls in pink dresses,
The girls dressed as boys,
And the happy German parents
In their curled, pastel wigs.
Clara makes her groan.
"That's my part!" she hisses,
Covering her eyes,
But looking up to cry—
"Oh, God! Her timing's off!"
I keep my eye on the stage
Trying with my attention
To keep Clara's slippers
From the next misstep or fall
Which the girl beside me wishes

To cause with her violent glare.
If this were New York or even
Some scene on television,
I'd fear for Clara's life.
But the girl's face slackens.
The false snow falls
Over the snowflake dancers.
Pierced by the haunting music
She is at last Clara.
If I could see in the dark
Below the edge of her skirt
I'd watch her feet arch.
Now she sways in her chair,
Hugging her arms, smiling.

Twenty-One

I used to dress as Juliet or Ophelia,
Put on the heavy mask of the actress,
Step out on the black, dizzying stage
Blinded by footlights, and recite my lines.
I wanted to tear the cloth off my breast
To show my ingenuousness to every stranger.
Look at my heart, I'd say, clotted, breaking.
But now I stay in the wings, fingering props,
The sword of silver paper, the plastic skull
Hamlet lifts from the papier-mâché grave.
Ophelia asks for her basketful of rue.
I hand it to her. She's pale and trembling,
Ready to loose her hair and float downstream
The way I used to when I played that scene,
The water under me, thrilling and cold.
Tonight I look at the rafters of the stage
Where curtains hang, moons are suspended.
What was it like to always be in love?
I'm pierced with longing to be twenty-one.
I'd like to walk breathless onto a stage
Of bare boards, foil stars above,
Wringing my hands over deathless passion—
And if the audience applauds, or yawns,
It doesn't matter. A meteor can't see
The gaseous atmosphere that makes it burn
Whirling and sparking on its way to earth.

Polio Epidemic, 1953

I blamed the cold water in the creek.
My legs were heavy, impossible to move
With flashing steps. I struggled from bed
At dawn to cross the green and gray tile
Dragging my right leg, forcing the left ahead
Until I reached my grandmother's porch,
Which faced the pasture and the red bull.
The bull bellowed when he saw me there,
His massive neck lowered, his horns bright.

I woke up in a ward of white cribs,
Glancing at other children, motionless
Behind the shadowy bars. Some merely slept.
Others had braces on their powerless legs.
I remembered my favorite story, "Sea Fairies."
A girl my age had turned into a mermaid
And dived at once into the turquoise sea.
I told myself that I was under water
Without the silver, necessary tail.
The heaviness of water must account
For my slowness as I left my crib
Hoping to find my mother or father.
All I found in the hall was an iron machine
Enclosing a grown-up woman, making her breathe.

I didn't go to second grade that fall.
A tutor came. I learned to spell "water."
I took spoonfuls of black medicine

To build my blood, and exercised my legs
With weights hanging from my bedroom door.
I couldn't bear to hear a sound repeated,
Chalk on a board, or steps on the basement stairs,
For noise made an ugly whisper in my ears
As if I were inhabited by someone
Murmuring: "You're going to die! Why didn't you?"

The Dance

The neighbor girl is posing on her porch
In her Nutcracker dress and pink dance slippers—
She's one of Clara's friends. Each night she goes
To practice in the auditorium.
I watch her mother take the last picture,
Then restless, my head aching, go upstairs
To find my photo album. The pages crack
As I look for photographs I took at nine
With my birthday present, a square Brownie,
And glued into this album years ago.
I find my best friend posed on the sidewalk
In her leotard, holding her baby brother.
Behind her, a woman younger than me now
Stands smoothing her blond page boy with one hand.
My friend's mother drove us to dance on Fridays
And waited with the other mothers on chairs
While we tried to lift our legs, move gracefully.
We bent and stretched. The mothers smoked, gossiped.
We saw them behind us in the big mirror
As we did our leg lifts. Some were pregnant.
Some had their hair in pincurls, others rollers.
The mirror made them seem so far away:
The shiny dance floor was a lake between us
And we were swans, drifting away from them.
We didn't need their clumsy hand-clapping,
Thoughtless praise of awkward pirouettes.
I used to look across illusory water
Wishing I could reach the vaporous shore

I moved toward as I danced, longing, dizzy.
Sweat filled my eyes. But just as I climbed up
Through quivering rushes on the distant side
And glimpsed the peaks, and spires, and domes of that
Perfected country, the piano stopped:
We heard the tap-dance class lining up
For their turn, clicking their steel toes.
I felt strange in the back seat going home
Breathing the smoke of Luckies, idly rubbing
My sore muscles as Elvis Presley sang
About the future when I'd dance with men.

Pole Vaulting

Our thin, tough bodies were identical
And when we threw ourselves one at a time
Across the bamboo pole at chest level
Any of us could break the last record.
I was a girl, but had the longest legs.
One brother was the tallest, one the lightest,
And one afraid of nothing, though his knees
Were always bandaged, and his palms scraped raw.
We practiced in the field behind our house,
And at our tournaments, called our mother
To act as referee and audience.
We ran and flung ourselves into the air,
Vaulting on the metal clothesline prop,
Trying to make our bodies horizontal,
And keep our feet from touching the bamboo.
Sometimes I thought I had wings on my heels
And if I let go when I was highest,
I'd fly above the roof and disappear.

Is this the same light body I could toss
Or bend backward, somersault, or cartwheel?
My brothers' sons are what my brothers were.
I hold them on my lap, and realize
I did fly off above the roof one day
And no one noticed. But where did I go?
Into the clouds, which swirled across my face.
I liked the heady sensation of flight
Though I was dropping downward half the way

To this Memorial Day, this picnic.
My brothers fry hamburgers, call their sons
In fathers' voices, and now I see
How they, too, disappeared in the bright air
As they cleared the high pole, and kept going.

Paradise

I roll up my sleeve,
Chatting with the nurse
Until I feel the sting
As she injects the pollen,
Johnson grass, Bermuda,
Mulberry, and olive,
Mixed with other traces,
Hair, dust, mold,
The essence of the world
Grown suddenly poisonous.
I used to lift mown grass
In heaps up to my face.
The scent made me dizzy
With childhood memory,
Sprinklers in the dark,
And ecstatic tumbles.
Now grass is dangerous.
All around me strangers
Sneeze like me, or take
Strangling gulps of air
Waiting for their shots.
As I pay at the window,
I recognize a friend
With stiff, swollen lips.
I know his throat is red.
He carries an inhaler
In his breast pocket.
We nod in the bright room

Full of desert sun
Where children play blocks
And parents read or doze.
I close the heavy door
On the air-conditioned clinic.
It's eighty degrees outside,
February in Tucson,
And up and down the street
The orange trees flower,
Filled with sipping bees.
It looks like Paradise—
The bright African daisies,
The magenta mountains,
The sky Sunday blue.

But as I walk along
I see the iron bars
Across the front windows
Of ordinary houses,
Bungalows, ranchers,
Tiled haciendas,
And know electric wires
Are hidden in clematis
To set off an alarm.
Once in my living room
Two police detectives
Told me it was hopeless.
I'd never see my things.

They'd never catch the thief
Who pawed my underwear,
And tore my Shakespeare,
Looking for hidden bills
Or a secret chamber
Cut into thick pages.
And so I raked the glass
Away from my oleanders,
Just beginning to bloom,
Their leaves inflammable,
And saw a blighted world
As if I looked through an arch
Or a high, grim gateway
On the other side of myself.
The mulberries I watered
Thrived in my backyard;
But every spring they puffed
Visible golden pollen
That drove me inside.
And the man dressed in white,
Strolling down my street
Under the gnarled olives
With a calm, dreamy face,
Might rob me, or kill
To get his heroin.
God didn't need to send
An angel to show the way
Outside of Paradise.

Adam and Eve could stay
And smell the fragrances
Until the snake arrived
For a little conversation
Before injecting venom.

Sorrow and Rapture

The April sun burned through the dirty glass.
My eyes burned. My wool skirt burned my knees.
Beyond the window of the city bus
As it turned up Forrest Hill, I couldn't see
Red brick, and frame, and budding maple trees,
But only the dark theater, where all alone
I'd watched *La Traviata* on the screen,
Surrounded by two-hundred empty seats.
I'd bought the ticket from a nun at school
For two dollars, and a written promise
Not to go home, or shopping, or idling.
I'd sunk back in the tattered velvet seat,
Glad to be out of Civics and History,
Breathing the odor of popcorn and licorice.
I wondered if they'd show the film for me,
Just me. I sat in the exact middle.
I was sleepy and warm. I hoped for color.
And then the sound track blared and leveled off.
The black-and-white singers floated far above me,
Magnified. Their singing made me dizzy.
The voices drew me forward on my seat,
And my face prickled with heat, my chest hurt.
I was more Violetta than I was myself.
I wore her satin gown. I loved Alfredo.
I raised her handkerchief to my own mouth.
The subtitles that flickered underneath
A passionate embrace, or stricken look,
Seemed more foreign to me than the music.

Then the bus stopped on top of the hill.
I looked over the roof tops of Peoria
Shaken with rapture. What town was this?
I saw the brewery, my high school, a steeple,
Slate-colored shingles, the glimmer of river,
And beyond, smokestacks of Caterpillar
Where the wire mesh gates had just opened on thousands
Of laborers with their metal lunch pails.
Still dazzled, I got off at my stop.
At home our maple almost cast a shadow
With its early buds, and I threw myself down.
No ants were stirring in the pale, cold grass
But here and there, in thick, green clumps,
Violets had bloomed, not yet choked by weeds,
Purple petals the size of fingernails.
I stroked the violets' heart-shaped leaves.
I looked at my hands. I stretched them in the sun.
I could remember the face of Alfredo,
Violetta's room, the view of Paris,
But not a single tune. I was tone deaf.
Still, I rolled over and over in the grass
Unable to speak, burning and longing,
As cars from the factories arrived on our street
And the smell of supper drifted out of doors.

Overnight in St. Louis

The plane I missed is still out there
Among the gleaming red and yellow lights
Of trucks and vans, and fragile private jets.
But the gate is closed. They won't let me on.
My tiny plane from Arkansas threw oil,
Making us late. Nothing can be done.
The next plane leaves tomorrow. A helpful agent
Types a message to Indianapolis
Where my husband paces and checks his watch again,
Thinking I'm almost home and in his arms.

The agent gives me a new boarding pass
For a morning plane. At last I catch the breath
I lost running with my heavy bag,
But my heart pounds over this suspension,
As if my life had broken, not a plane.
I thought I could go anywhere I wished
The way my father used to when he flew
This way and that across the Midwest,
Davenport to Springfield at any hour
Or up to Peoria to avoid a storm.

The waiting area is nearly empty.
I peer through the window's safety glass.
My plane still sits at the end of the locked ramp
In a night bright as a garden. The flares,
The flashing towers, the brilliant searching beams
Make me think of the great Exposition

My grandmother visited with surprise
Eighty years ago, 1904.
She saw ephemeral lights, an Arabian city
Built on the plain beside the ignored river.

She walked aghast through the illusions
Holding hands with her mother and father.
She never could recall what she had seen
Inside the Palaces of Science and Art,
But she never forgot the force of all that light
As if the stars had fallen in Missouri.
I might be staring at the same scene,
A fairy-like projection from somewhere,
Perhaps a heaven of long-dead stars
Apparently real, shining as hard as ever.

All airport lights are useless to me now.
I can't get home tonight by any route.
I watch my plane move away at last.
If I were on board, I'd close my eyes
For that little jolt from ground to air.
In thirty-three minutes I'd resume my life
With hugs and talk. Instead I look up.
Beyond the lights, the sky is immense.
A few planes dare to cross at intervals
Farther and farther apart, like canoes at sea.

Old Women Under the Olive Trees

One apartment tower makes a shadow
Halfway to the other. The pool's between.
I cross the crackling grass to find Minnie,
Who likes to sit under the olive trees
With other women in their seventies
Every Sunday. They don't go to church
But idly watch the families who do,
Fathers and mothers from the first floor
(Where children are allowed) pulling a boy
With combed hair past his swimming friends,
Or showing off a daughter in anklets.
Each woman sits in her own folding chair.
I smile and rest in the grass at Minnie's feet,
Show her the bread I've baked, and nod hello
To her three friends. I've met them all before.
They know I'm her childless daughter-in-law.
They hardly look at me as they talk on,
Remembering their lives before they moved
To Arizona, wishing they'd left sooner.

I lie back. I can see a mountain top
Past the flat roof of the highest tower,
A purple edge against shimmering sky.
Betty claims she never saw a mountain
Until she was sixty. She hates the snow.
She won't go back to visit Illinois.
Louise was mugged twice in Philadelphia,
And was afraid to answer her front door.

Martha buried her husband in the rain.
She thought her empty house would float away.
I feel the stiff grass under my fingers,
And an ant trickles across my bare foot.
I close my eyes but the light burns through.
I seem to see three lives in front of me
Like matches struck one-by-one in the dark,
Betty looking down her snowed-in driveway,
Louise weeping, a bruise on her forehead,
Martha pulling on a second sweater
Though the chill is in her heart, not the air.

An airplane drills across the cloudless sky.
I look up at the silver olive leaves,
Feeling the curve of earth under my back.
I hear the rustle of the Sunday paper
As each woman returns to her section,
Minnie trading Sports for Betty's Leisure.
I used to drive up to Baltimore
To visit Minnie in her gloomy row house.
I'd hear neighbors quarreling through the walls,
See cockroaches along her countertops,
And know she sat alone by the window
Looking out at nothing, her old cat dead.
She wanted to die, too, her life hopeless.
She made me wonder what I was, might be.
Now she smiles and chatters as if transformed
Though her heart is older, her hands stiffer.

I look at the curled white hair on her brow.
Years and years are piled into her head,
The farm she hated, her Italian father
Who pulled her out of school to scrub floors,
Sisters and brothers already dead,
And the house she lived in forty years, then left,
Dresser drawers of broken combs and dust
Cleaned out at last, and sold at an auction,
All of it inside her, packed hard like snow
So that the flakes have lost their starry shapes.

Heaven

Talk floats. Rain covers the windows.
We're driving north to show Mount Vernon
To my mother-in-law and her niece, Mary.
In the back seat Minnie and Mary sigh
As both of them recall Miss Ambrose
Who died at ninety-five last summer.
Mary is sixty, short and diabetic.
Minnie is seventy-four, her memory sharp.
Miss Ambrose lived in Minnie's neighborhood
Until she moved away at eighty-eight
Unable to dress or push the toaster down.
Minnie tells me she was called Birdy
And makes me see the ordinary yard
Crowded with birds, red wings, black wings,
Strange crests, odd scolding cries
Mixed up with trills, and whippoorwill songs.
Birdy hung feeders on the clothesline.
She filled three bird baths in the hot summer
And kept a house for every size of bird.

Minnie talks about her last visit
At a cousin's house near railroad tracks:
Birdy rocked on the porch; her cousin fed
The train-yard crows to keep her entertained,
But nothing satisfied her, she'd grown bitter
Knowing she'd die and go at once to heaven
Where soulless birds were not allowed to enter.
Mary gasps at this view of heaven.

She's Italian. She says her rosary at night.
She knows heaven will be full of birds.
She describes it to us and I see
The bright blue sky and gold halos
Around the heads of smiling multitudes,
Lions and birds, and saints in white robes.
Minnie says nothing. There's a sly
Flicker in her eyes when I glance back.
She only believes in her funeral. She owns
Her own grave plot in Baltimore,
Near her father and mother, and she worries
Conniving relatives may steal it from her.
We have promised to send her back in a coffin
Of walnut, with luxury satin lining.
Mary shakes her head over Miss Ambrose,
Wishing she'd known the truth about heaven.

And then the talk subsides. I hear the rain
Ping on the roof of the car; the wipers click.
I remember my own childhood picture of heaven.
God was endless, a purple ring of smoke
Worshipped by crowds sitting on bleachers;
Such a bleak scene was easy to give up
Without a crisis and without regret.
Yet I can envy Mary's pretty heaven.
I'd rather have the lambs, the golden horns,
And go for long flights across the clouds
With my muscular wings than plan to lie

Three feet under the heavy Baltimore clay
In my best dress, like Minnie, who can make
My husband speechless with her grasp of details
About embalming or the price of headstones;
She claims she won't miss anything on earth.

And now we have arrived. We all raise
Umbrellas against the soft September rain,
And wander through George Washington's gardens.
Minnie is bored. She only came to please us.
Mary exclaims at the colors of the flowers,
The many shades of bushy four o'clocks
Just like the ones at home she calls
"Marvel of Peru." The lawns shine
Under a million drops of water, and birds
Peck and sing and fly above our heads.
Miss Ambrose would have been delighted,
I almost say. But I don't say it.
I know I'm going to Birdy's empty heaven
Where no birds fly, where all day
She rocks on a porch beneath a blank sky
And nothing she loves ever comes in sight.

The Invalid in the Window

One November I walked in the fine rain.
I held my green umbrella. I thought and hummed.
I looked into the charming, yellow rooms
Where lamps glowed against the gray weather,
Imagining I lived in this or that house,
The one with the piano, or next door
Where someone owned a little rocking chair.
I walked to the end of town. I thought I saw
The heaving sea. Its cliffs were misted tree-tops,
The distant roar of trucks its mighty waves.
Then I turned back into my inland town
Singing to myself. But all at once the blur
Of pink and blue behind a picture window,
Which I glanced boldly into as I strolled,
Resolved itself into a woman's shape.
She was immensely old. She seemed already dead
Although she stared at me, motionless on her bed,
Which had been cranked to let her sit and look
Out her front window at the passers-by.
Quickly I dipped the rim of my umbrella
But too late, for I had entered her
With the same indifferent thrust of mind
That took me into mansions or made a sea.
I felt the stiff sheets up around my neck.
I couldn't move my numb and bluish feet.

Elegy for Helen Waddell

She was a scholar—she shivered as she read
And felt the shock of being someone else.
She looked up, confused, rubbing her head
When Latin words pierced her like a bell—

Or she pierced them to reach an agony
Fresh as a packet of needles in her hand.
Nothing surprised her, not the bomb's debris,
The Roman urns discovered in the sand

When London brick toppled, nor the fall
Of Europe. She had stood on walls before
To watch barbarian armies glitter and sprawl.
Her mind lit darkness like an open door.

But through that door another entered, too:
Amnesia, with his bland, devouring crew.

March

Upstairs my husband types our wills,
Pressing the keys with one finger.
The sound makes eerie counterpoint,
To all the birds, newly arrived.

We have assigned our house and cats.
We've looked at our insurance forms.
The will must be typed perfectly.
The drafts are growing at his feet.

The typing stops, then starts again
While birds sing loudly in our tree,
And I remember how each March
The priest put on his purple stole.

March was Lent, the time of mourning.
I thought that it would never end.
I wished to be grown-up, and gone
To sunny places, warmer lands.

Now March is short, but just as cold.
The birds fly off to make new nests
In trees they've never seen before.
I shudder at the tapping keys.

They strike the music of bequests,
Of bonds, executors, and graves—
Black notes across a legal page,
Meant to be played when we are dead.

Trees, Trees

Neither catalpa-tree nor scented lime . . .
—William Butler Yeats

I thought the only trees I'd ever know
Were oaks and maples, but my list of trees,
The trees I recognize by bark or leaf,
Grows in spite of myself. Yeats's limes
Are really lindens, those familiar trees
That grow along my own, ordinary street
To scent the spring with spicy restlessness.
And Proust's acacias are the ferny locusts
That spread their yellow pollen everywhere.
There's one next door. It's near a sycamore,
Marred, peeling, spotted like a dog—
The European plane that lines the streets
Of romantic villages in Provence.
And the old cigar tree, which every summer
Littered the alley with its ugly seeds,
Turns out to be the lovely catalpa,
A tree that, blooming, takes my breath away—
A tree like a cloud or snowy mountain top—
Though as a child I hardly noticed it.
I must be looking at a tree right now,
Which some day shall be lit by memory,
The dogwood on my lawn, the Norway pine,
Though, close-up, they seem less valuable
Than the olive tree I left in Arizona,
Or the flaming sumac of a Southern wood.
I remember walking in that autumn wood
Holding hands with my husband, dreaming
That the whole future stretched before us—

As if the trees went on and on, and sumac
Burned passionately to show the way.
That was years ago, but we've kept on
Beyond the red fringe of scrub sumac,
To reach the taller, darker, nameless trees
That sway above the disappearing path.

Living Apart

I leave our house, our town, familiar fields
Below me at takeoff when I fly to you
Deep in these shadowed mountains. Now at dawn
I wake to the horse-clop of passing carriages
As if I'd passed through time as well as space.
Yesterday we saw an Amish farmer
Bearded and calm, stroking his horse's mane
Under a flaming maple as he watched
Hang gliders drifting down from Hyner View.
We stopped to watch them, too. I was amazed
To see men falling toward the scarlet tree tops
On outspread wings. That's when I grabbed your hand
To tell myself we were alive and human
Not lost in hell, which must resemble this—
A place where souls from many centuries
Stand side by side, united but unhappy,
To watch the angels fall from fiery mountains.

Good People

The sight of all these people in the street
Heading a dozen directions, in puffy coats,
Icelandic hats, in boots or rubber shoes,
All walking stiffly on the melting ice,
Necks bent against the wind, makes me giddy.
If we could hear each other think, the noise
Would shatter glass, break the best hearts.
A businessman in a camel overcoat
Passes a red-haired girl with a yellow scarf,
And neither will ever see each other again

Or see me standing outside the florist's.
I'm buying flowers for my mother, who lies
In the hospital with a blood clot in her vein,
Almost recovered. I saw her yesterday
And through the doors of other rooms I glimpsed
Face after face I didn't recognize,
Twisting on wet pillows, or watching TV.
How accidental my existence seemed—
I might have sat beside some other bed.
I might have loved that man in blue pajamas

Or kissed the silent child in the metal crib
Receiving a transfusion, as I did once,
Thirty years ago to save my life.
Then a car honks. A woman jostles me.
I stare in wonder down the crowded street.
I could be part of one of these strangers

Breathing hard in the cold, Kentucky air,
That tall man with gnarled, shaky hands
Or that heavy woman, or part of someone dead
Who thought that life was choice, not accident.

Unfinished Bridge
at Encarnation, Paraguay

I

This is the same photograph. Nothing's changed.
I remember pulling it out of the chemicals,
Pleased with so many shades of black and grey.

"Study in Fog," I think I called it then—
I captured the arches of the ruined pilings
Down to the glistening shore, and on the water

Glimpsed in pieces through the keyhole arches,
Seven boats, one of the boats a ferry,
All its windows reflected across ripples.

I liked the silvery mud in the foreground,
The sharpness of form and texture, the faint line
Of another country at the horizon,

Argentina, a smear of ash on pearl.
I remember the two soldiers with rifles
Who came toward me from the customs shed

Warning me away. But it seemed comic.
How could an unbuilt bridge mean anything
To the military? But I had snapped the shutter.

I wanted concrete details for my novel
Set in Paraguay in the nineteenth century,
And here was the past, decorative, exotic,

Still visible in the spacious present.
I photographed the men in wooden carts
Who craned to watch me, flicking their long whips

Over the hunched necks of plodding bullocks.
I snapped the row of silent, sad-eyed women
In line for the ferry. It rained for three days.

Oranges rotted. The mud was thick and red
And stained the soles of my white tennis shoes
Permanently, as if I walked in blood.

II

I lift the photograph in its plastic frame
Off my wall, and wipe away the dust.
I haven't looked at it in years. It's hung
Unnoticed by people entering my house,
A study in perspective, almost abstract.
I look at the grainy mud, some hewn blocks,
And for the first time observe how the concrete
Has eroded halfway up the black pilings
As if the dangerous Alto Paraná,
Over which the train itself is ferried,
Swallows the unstable shore at flood time.

I remember the impenetrable gloom
Of the winter sky above dripping palms,
How I rode in a horse-drawn taxi, ate *chipa*,
And took my careful notes and photographs
Thinking reality was made of details
That might be woven, like Nañduti lace,
Into a perfect, geometric pattern.
The afternoon I took this photograph
I bought a piece of lace in the market
From a toothless woman who spoke Guaraní.
She talked, pointing at the lace in my hand,
Until I smiled and nodded, moving away.
I guessed she had described her technique
For making the abstraction of a web
Out of common thread, knotted and pulled
Into a symmetry no spider equaled.
But now, drawing her face up from memory,
I see a death's head under her bright scarf
As if she'd really told me something else—
That after lace makers had sketched the webs
Spun across the feathery tips of grasses
And re-created beauty, the spiders dined
Greedily on the flies caught in the strands.

Still staring at my own good photograph
Made out of light with the correct f-stop,

My eyes burn to think of my ignorance.
These arches, mud holes, ripples, hazy clouds
Are more than elements of composition.
That ferry shuttling over to Posadas
Carried the same Argentine citizens,
Mothers, fathers, children learning to read,
Who began to disappear by the family
Just as I stood there with my camera—
Swept out of life for the wrong politics
And into hidden graves in the countryside.

This is a photograph of the River Styx
And my frame is crammed with the invisible.
Now ten years later I can see the throng
Gathered on the far shore, wringing their hands—
A mother murdered after hours in labor
Searches for the baby she has never seen;
A husband calls his wife, longing to touch
The thick braid that once hung down her back;
Smothered children recite the alphabet
Puzzled to find their lessons at an end . . .
What are they doing there? Why am I here?
Sight is not sight, when under the visible,
Sky, shore, water, limestone, boats,
The molecules are swirling, nothing's real,
And eyes are blindfolds, art embroidery—

But as I stare again at that ruined bridge
I want to finish it, and let the dead
Come back, shouting, across the dark river
Of uncertain current and piranha fish,
To tell the truth about the human heart
Buried inside each chest, so deep and strange.